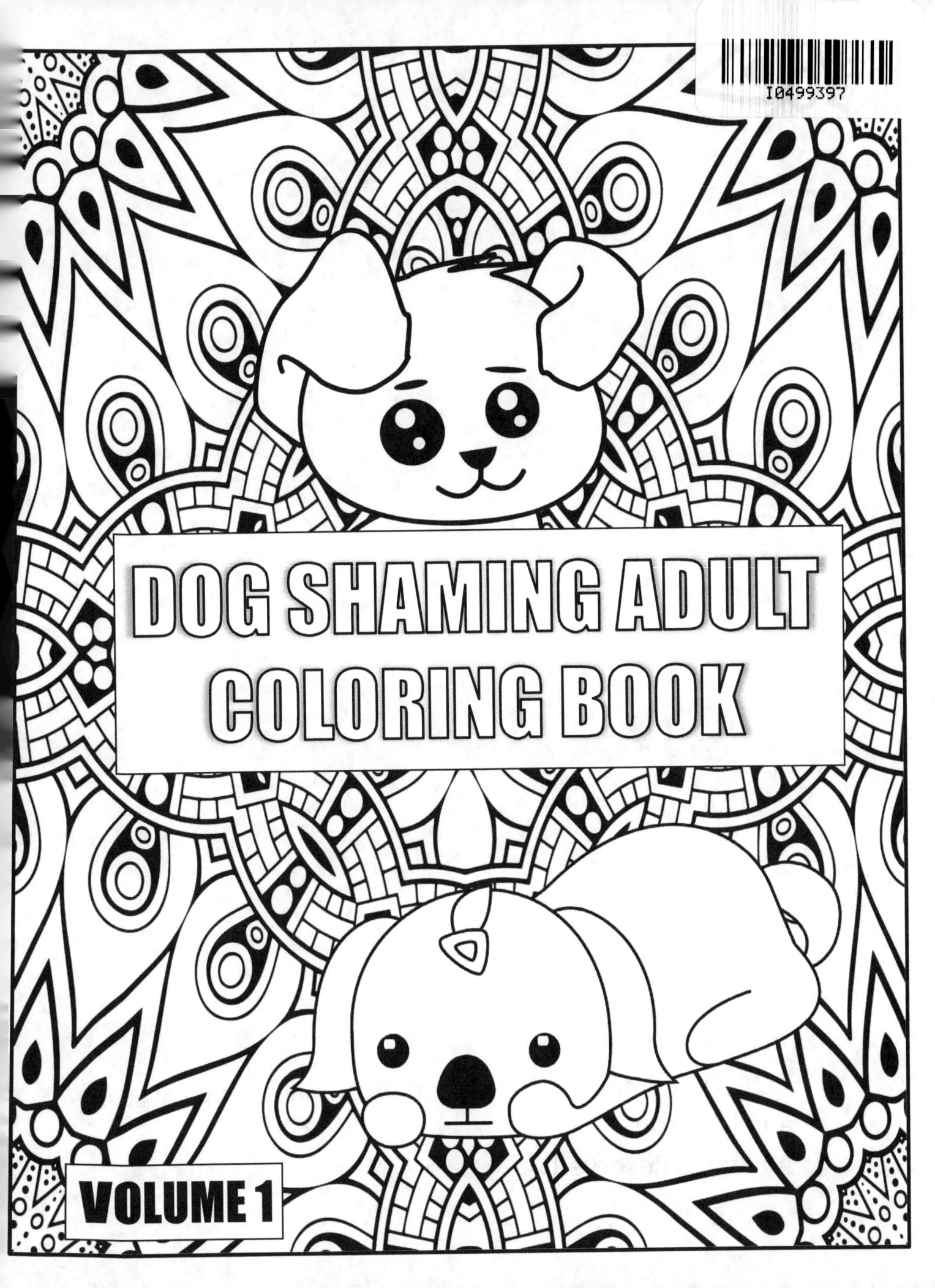

©2019, Animal Fun Press, and its affiliates and assigns and licensors
All Rights Reserved.

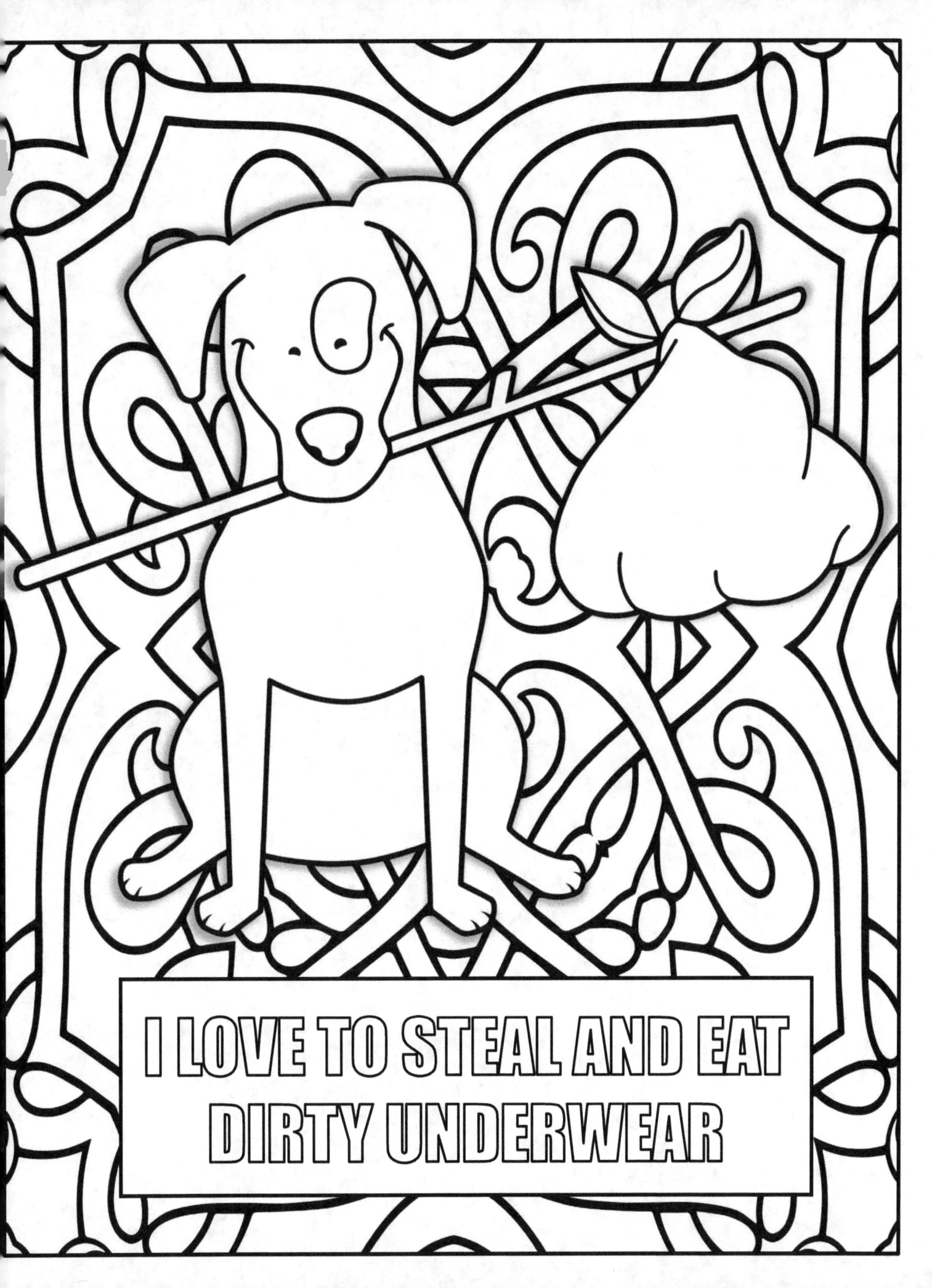

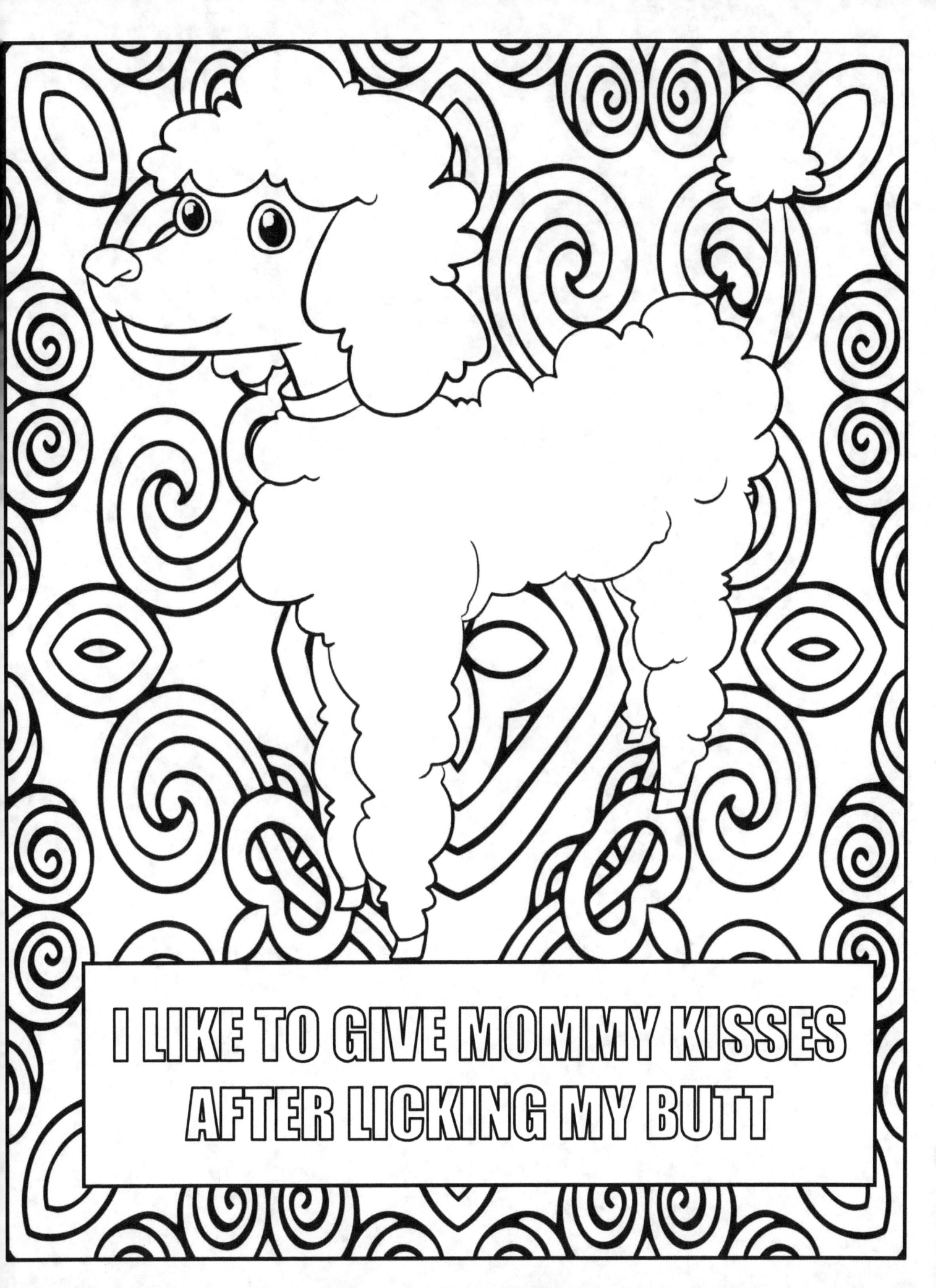

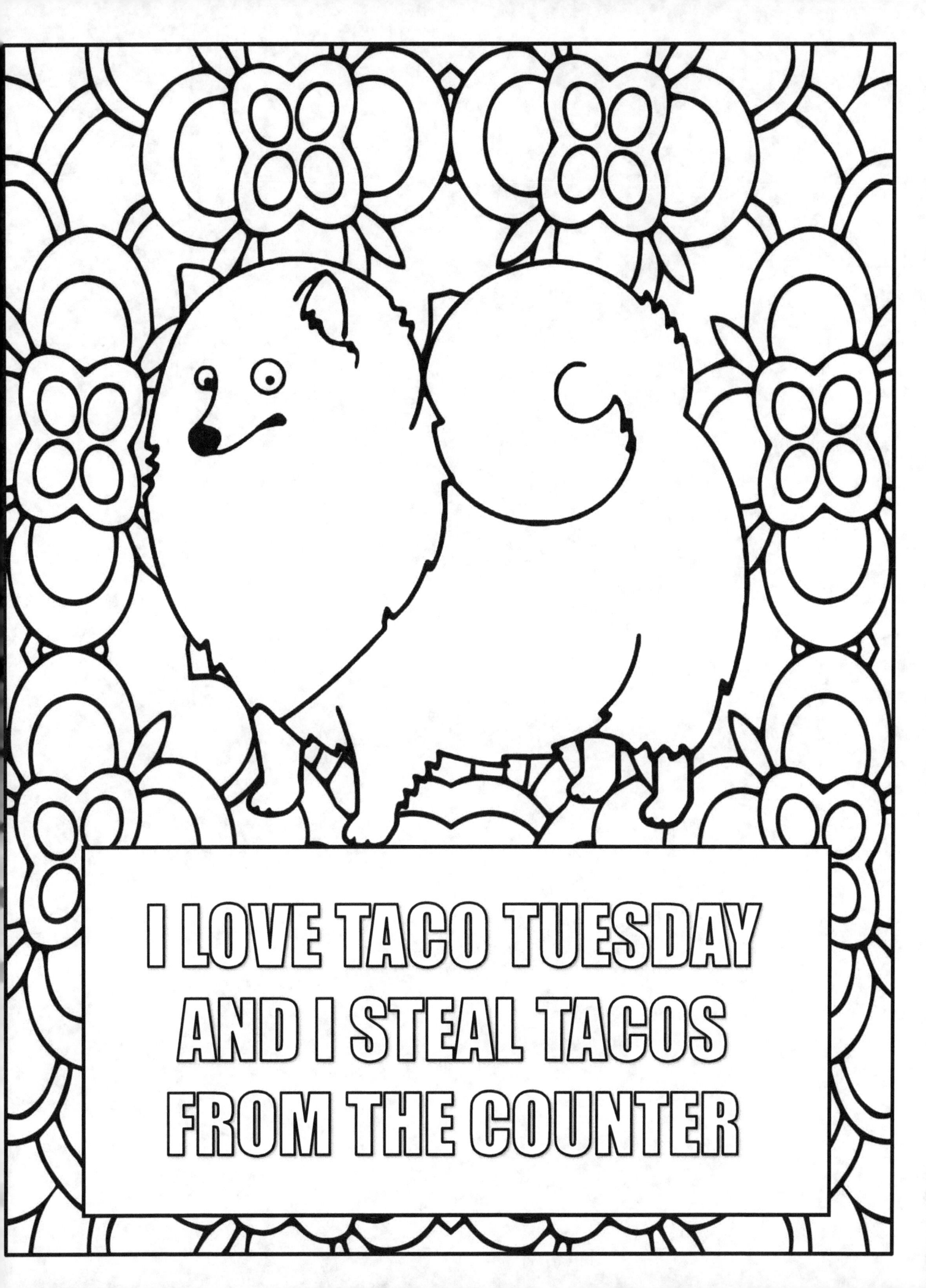

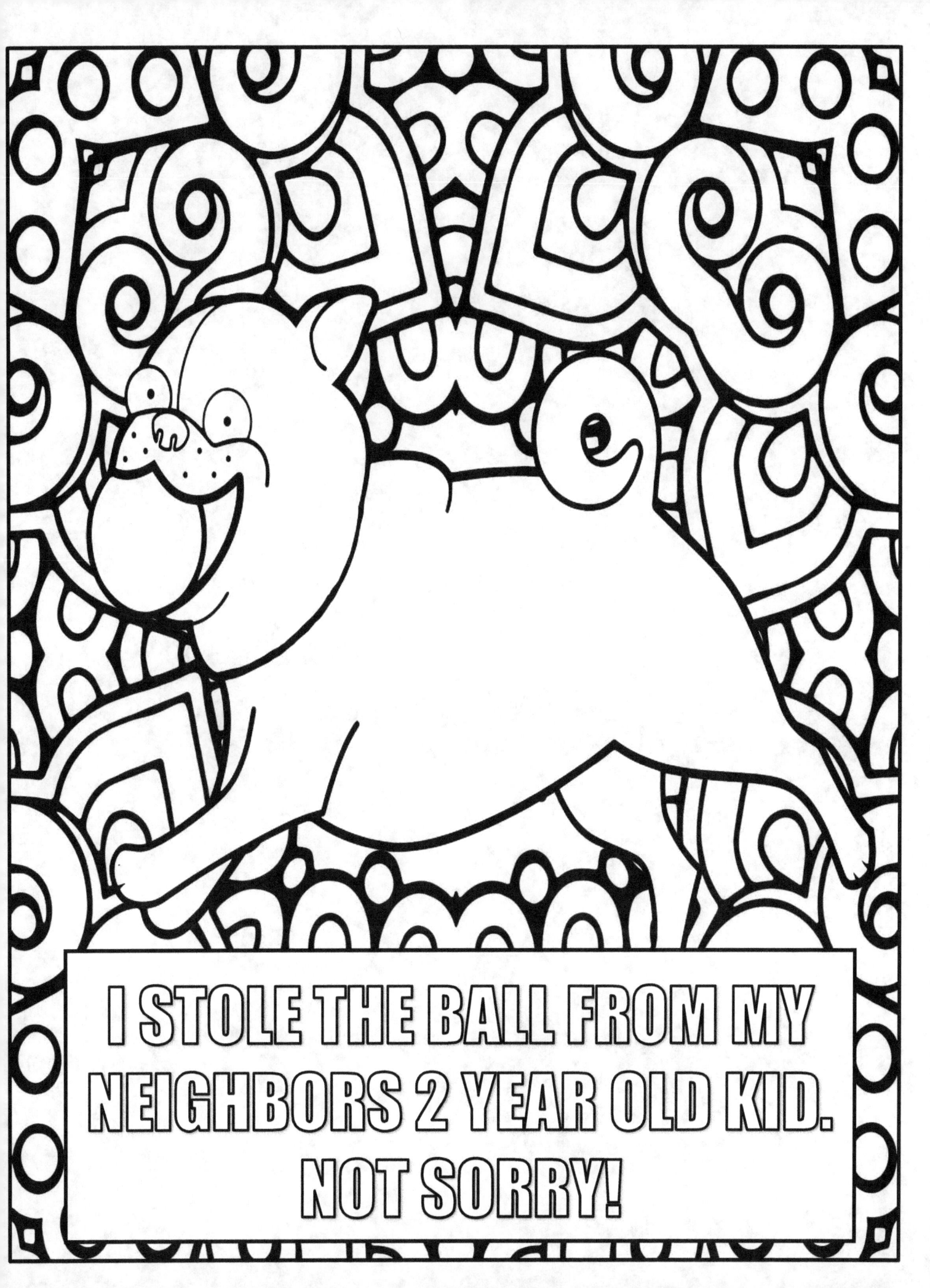

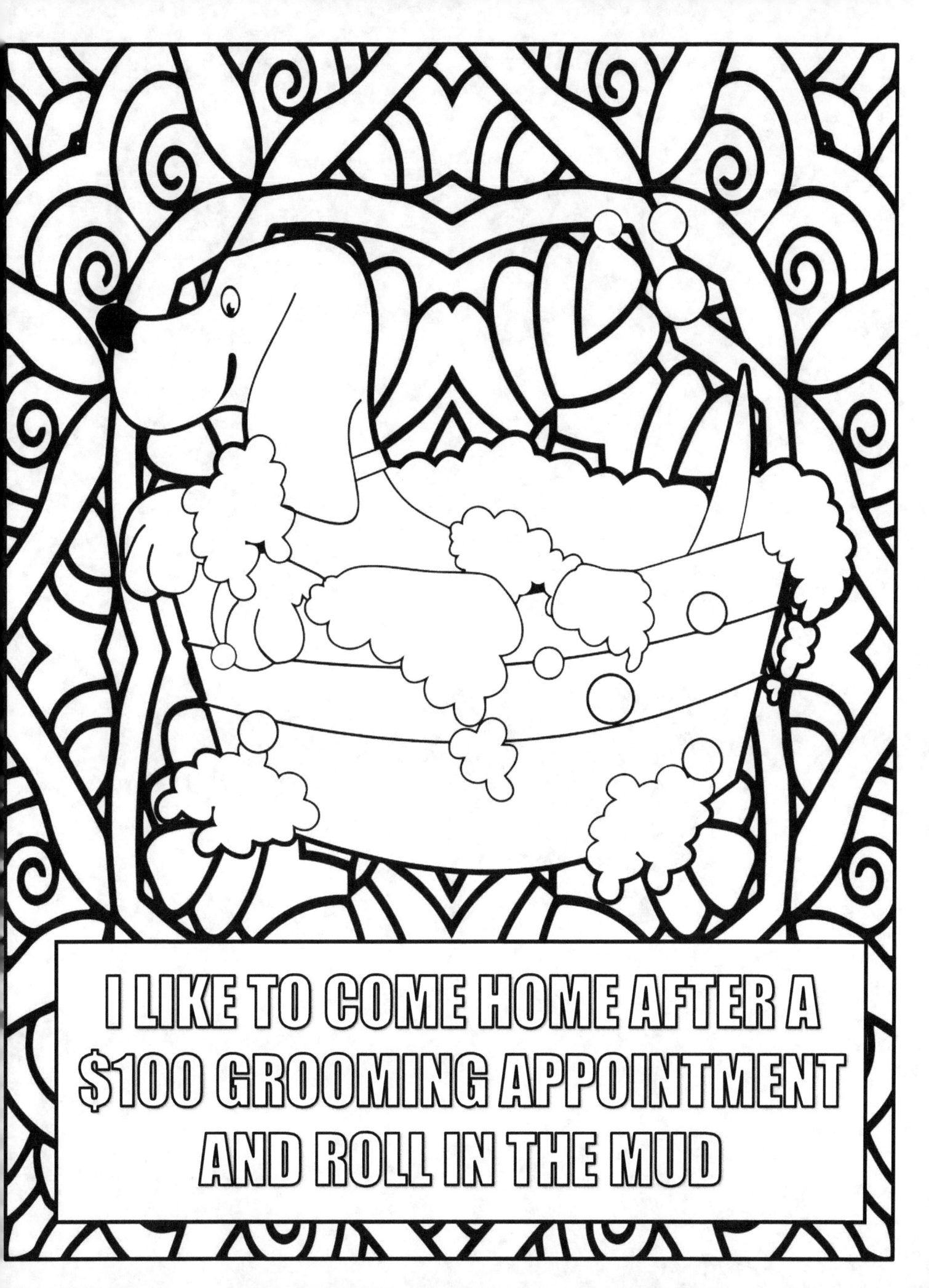

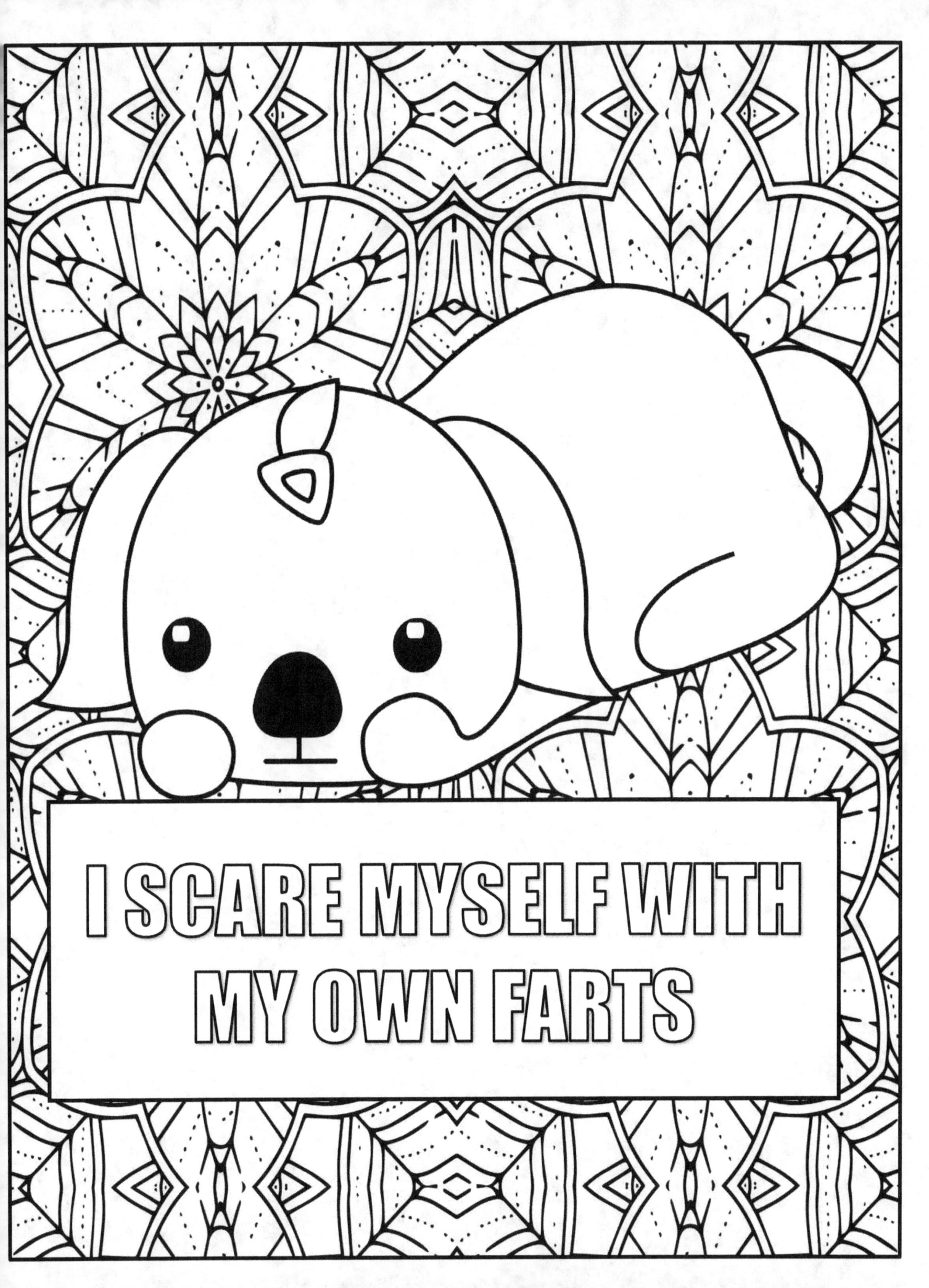

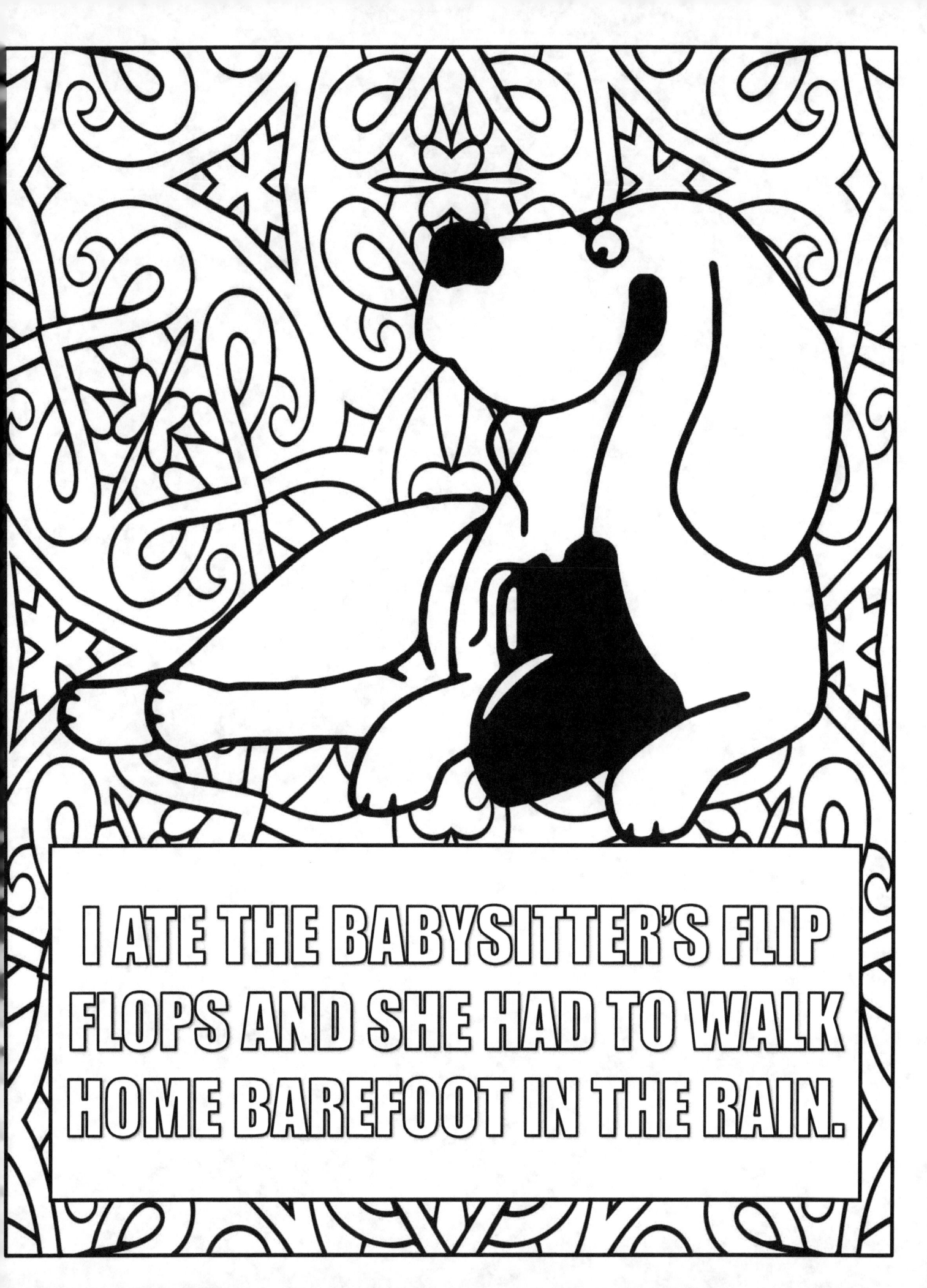

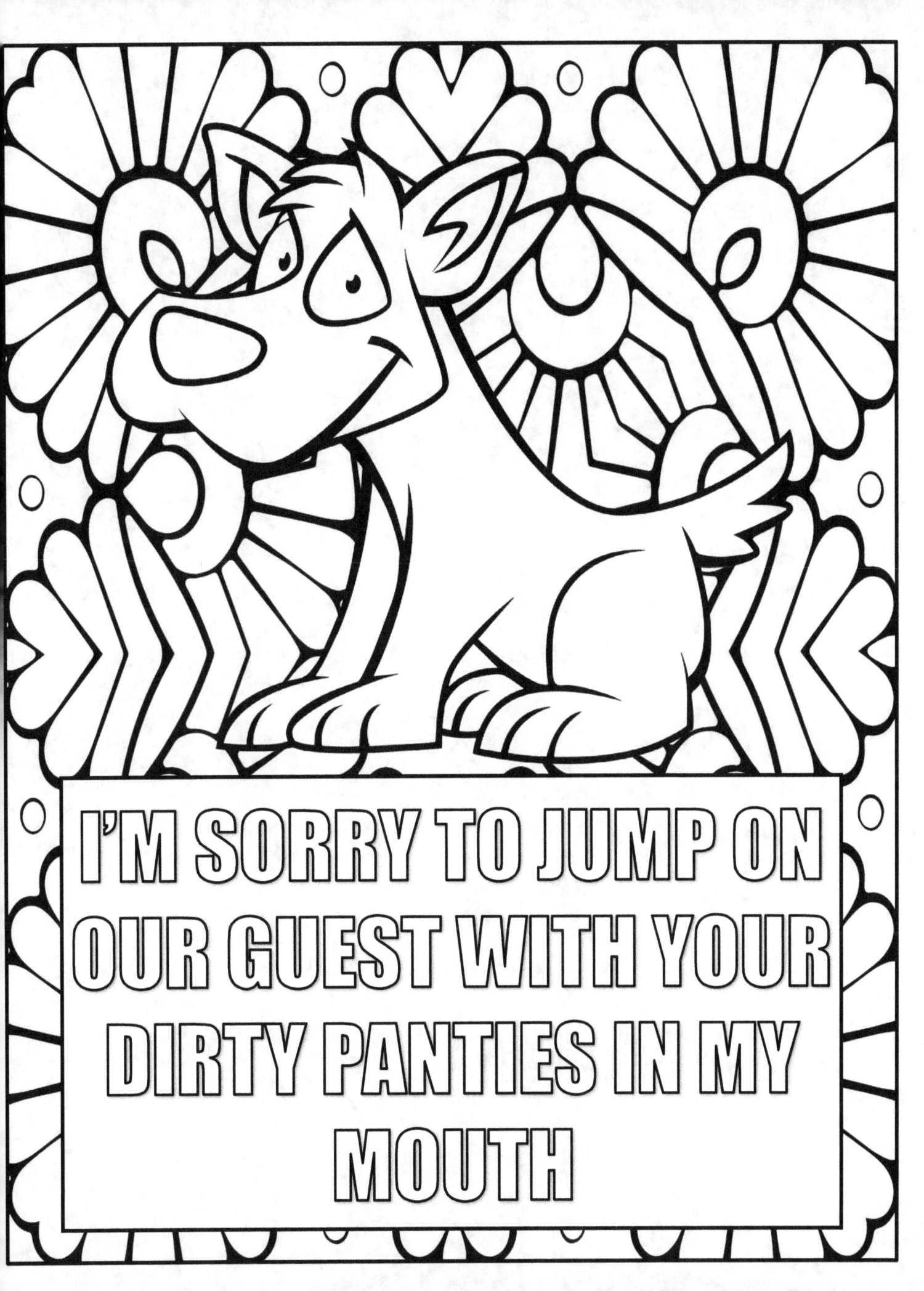

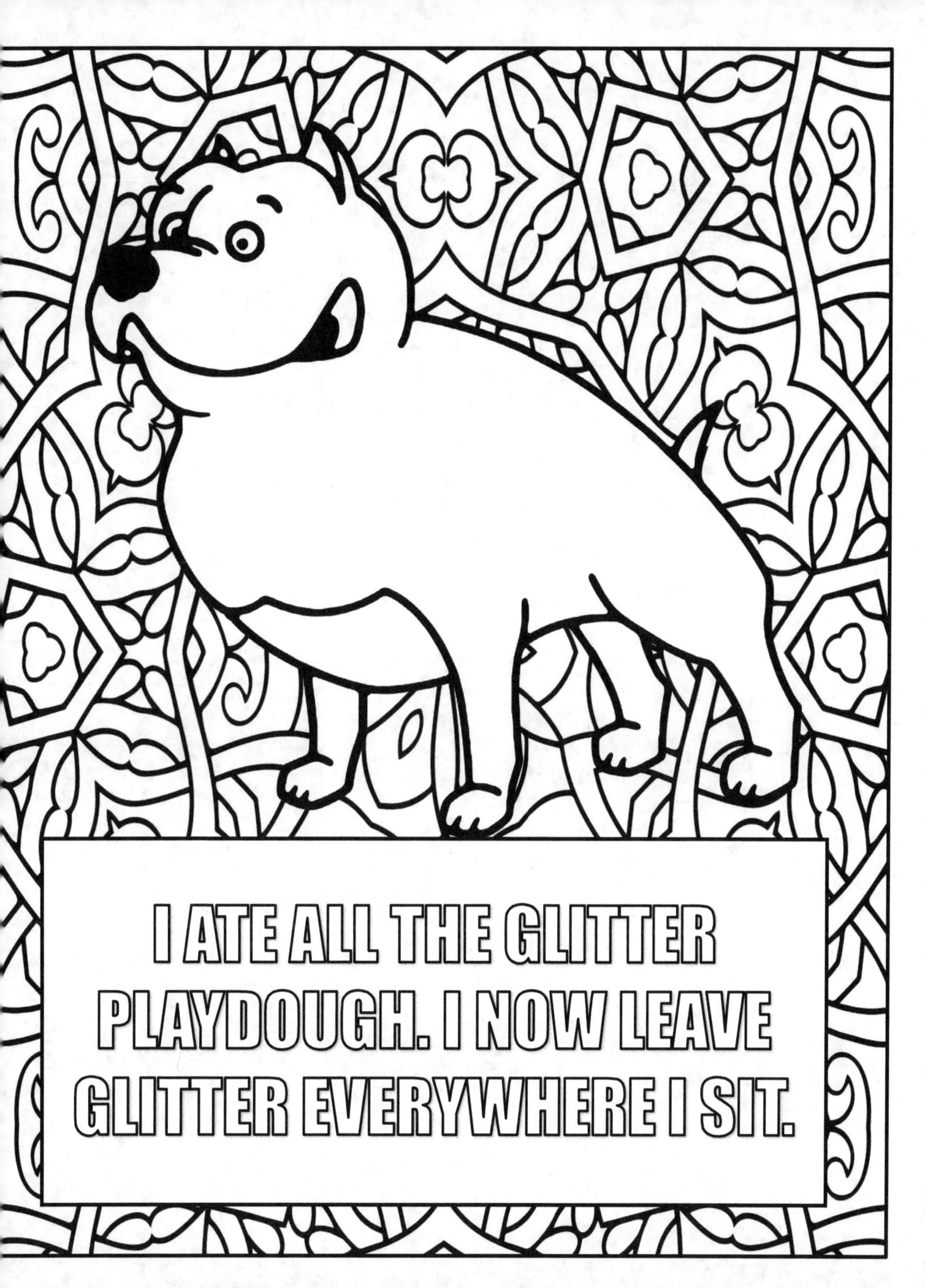

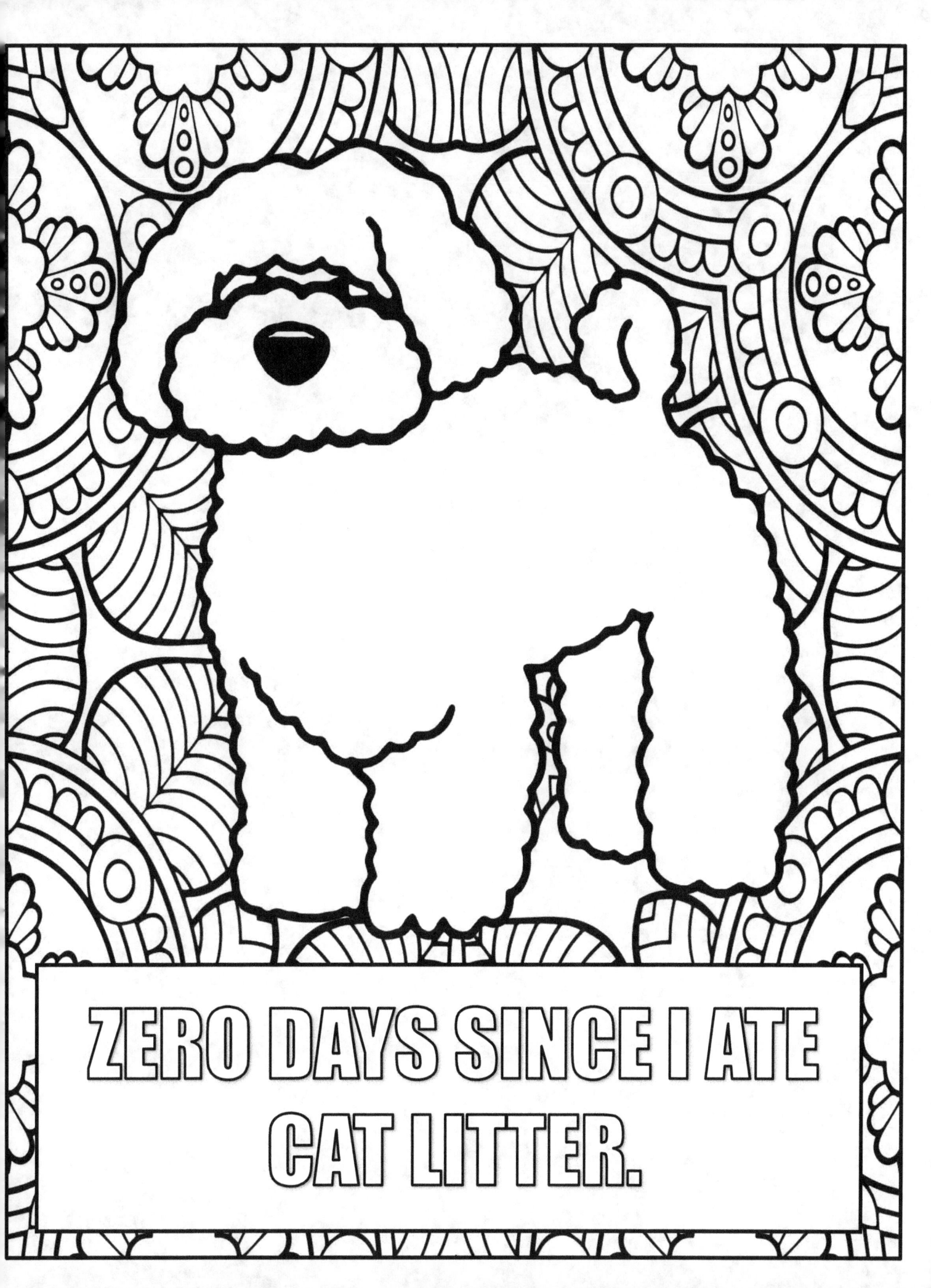

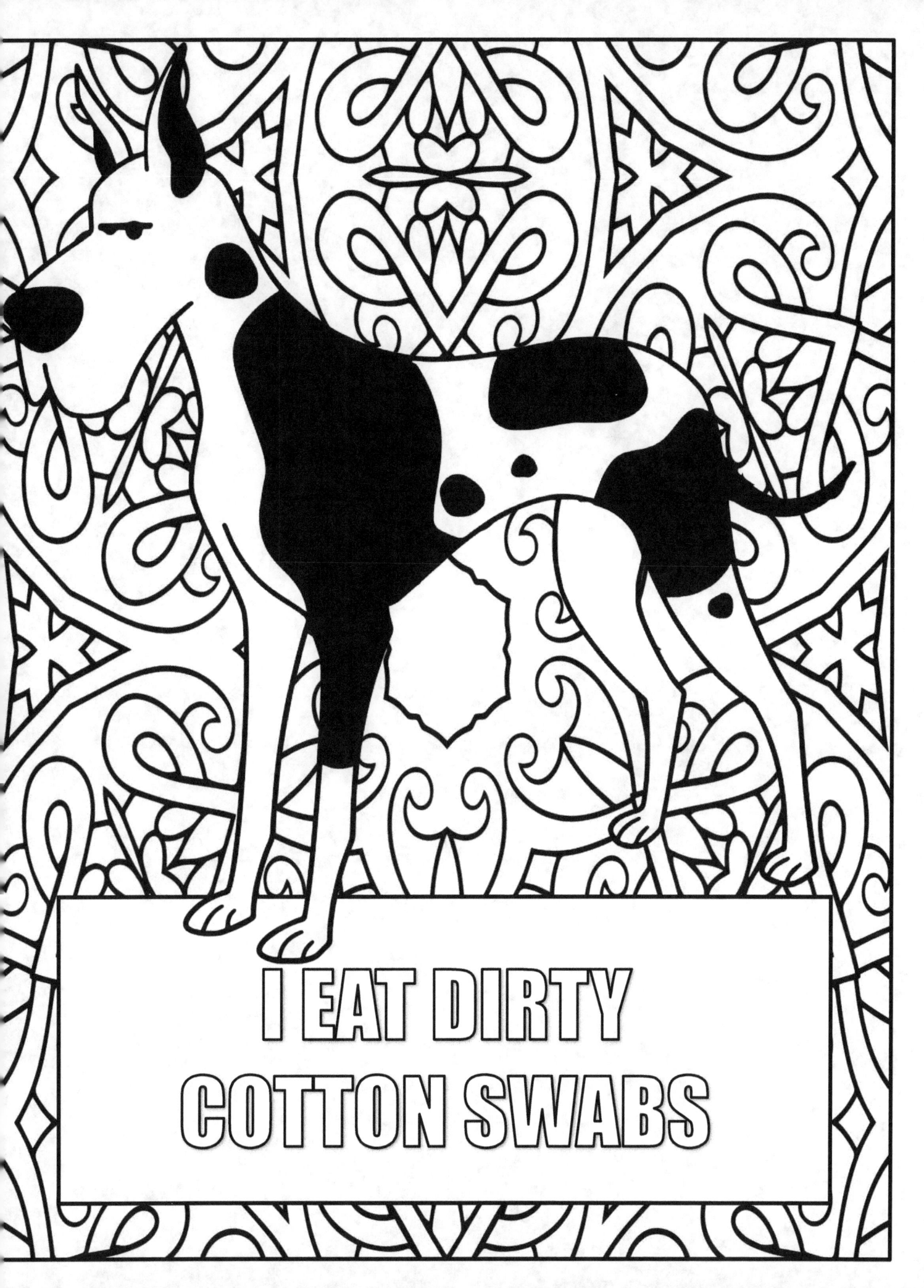

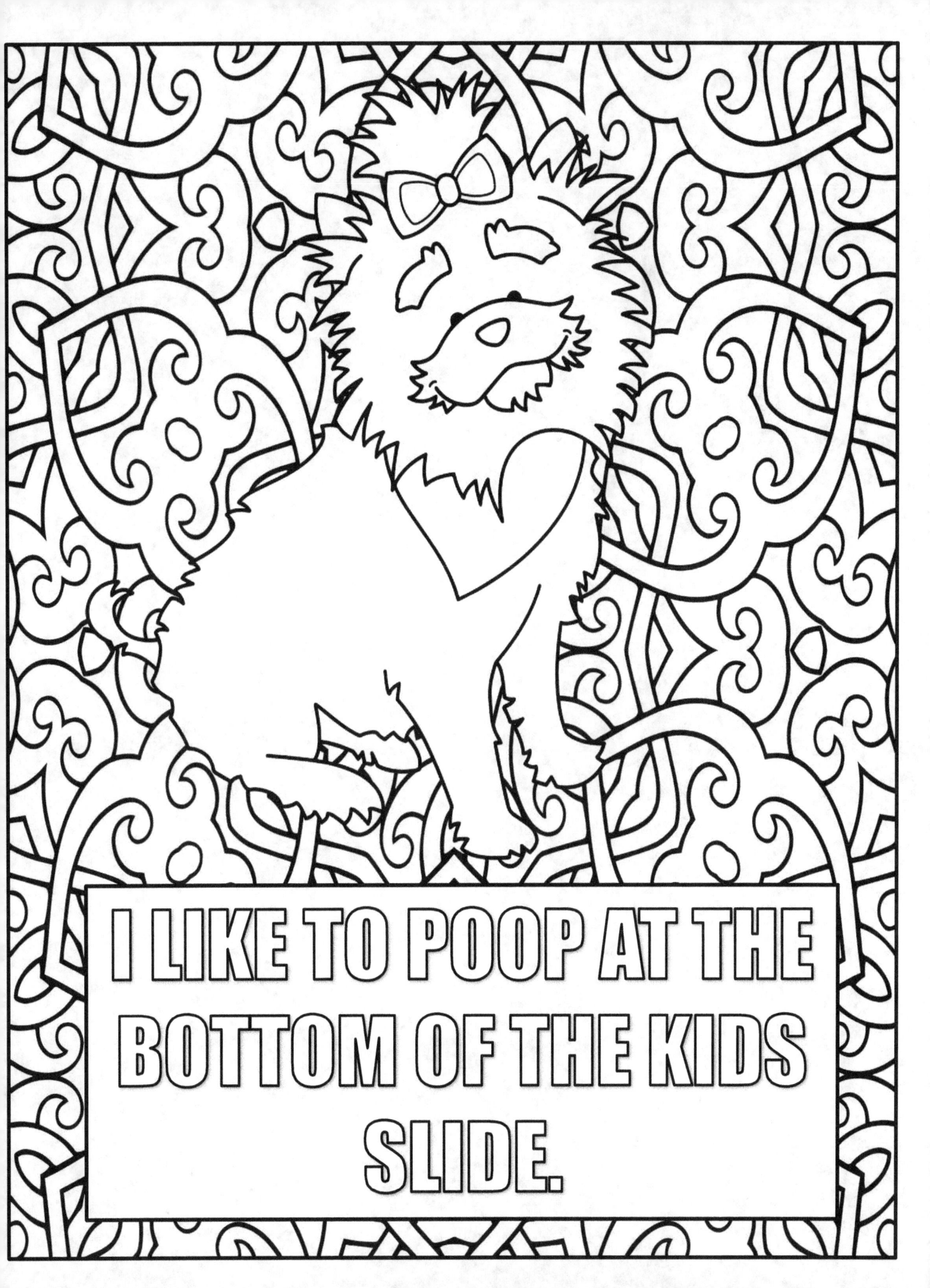

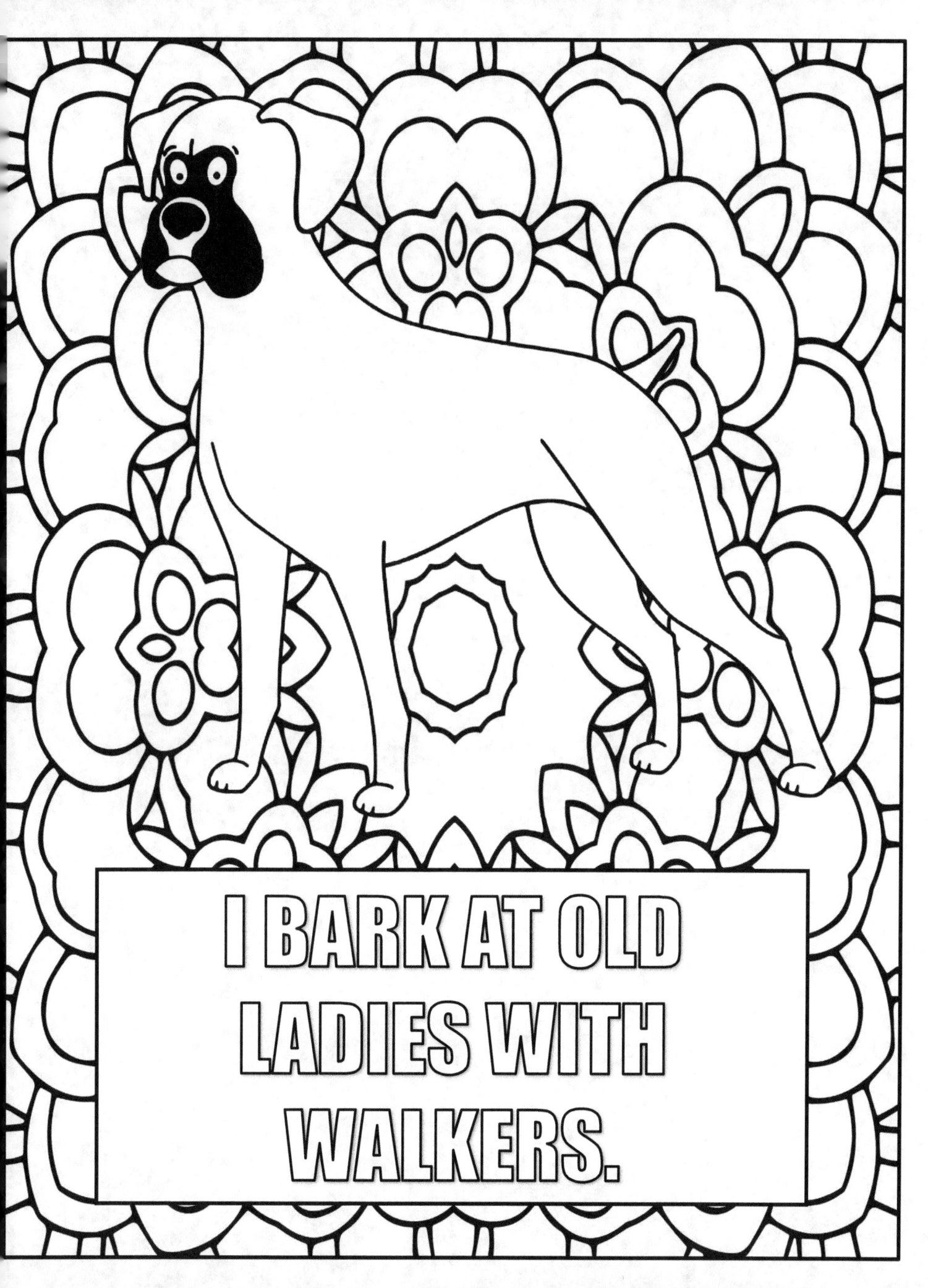

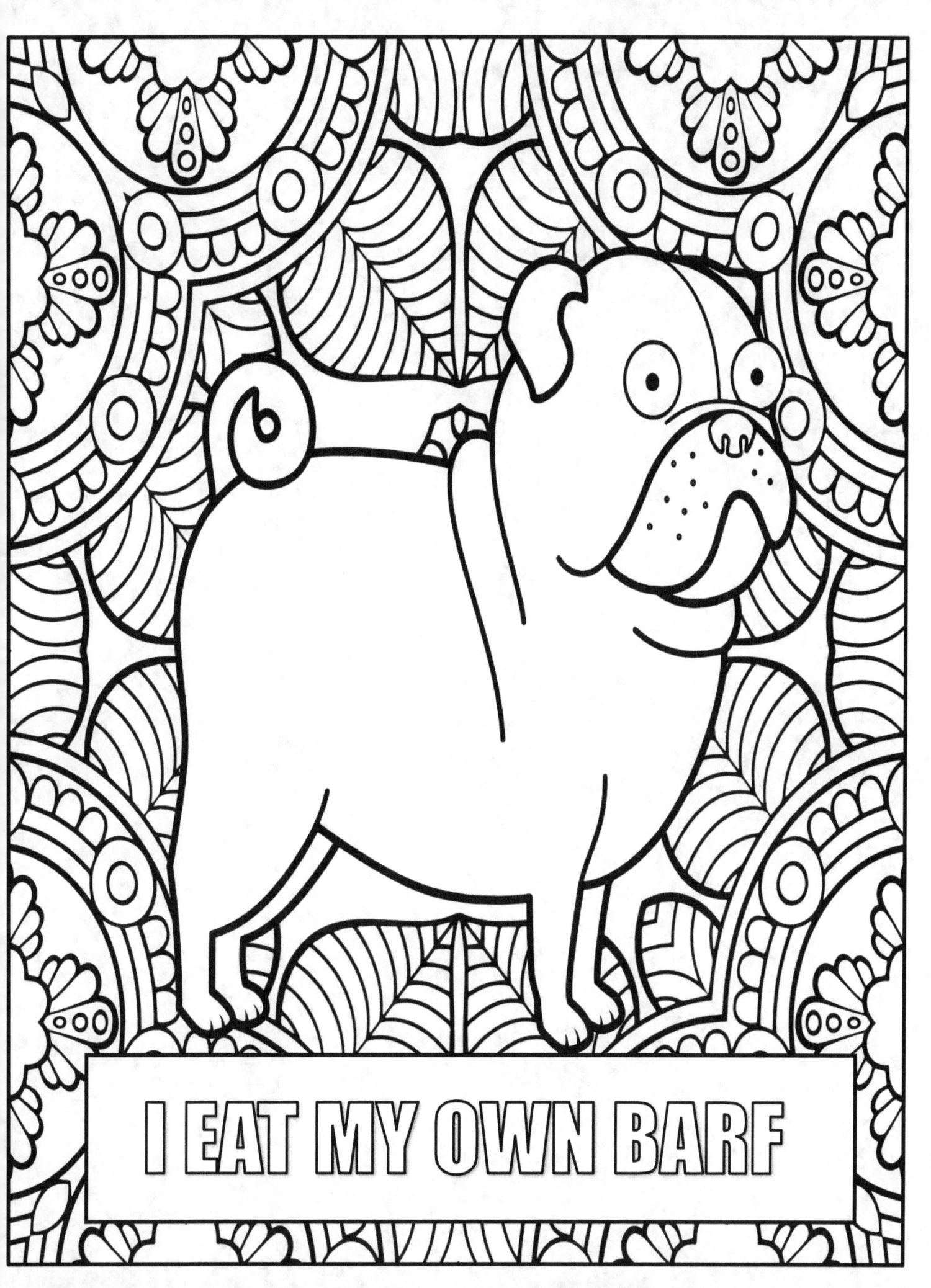

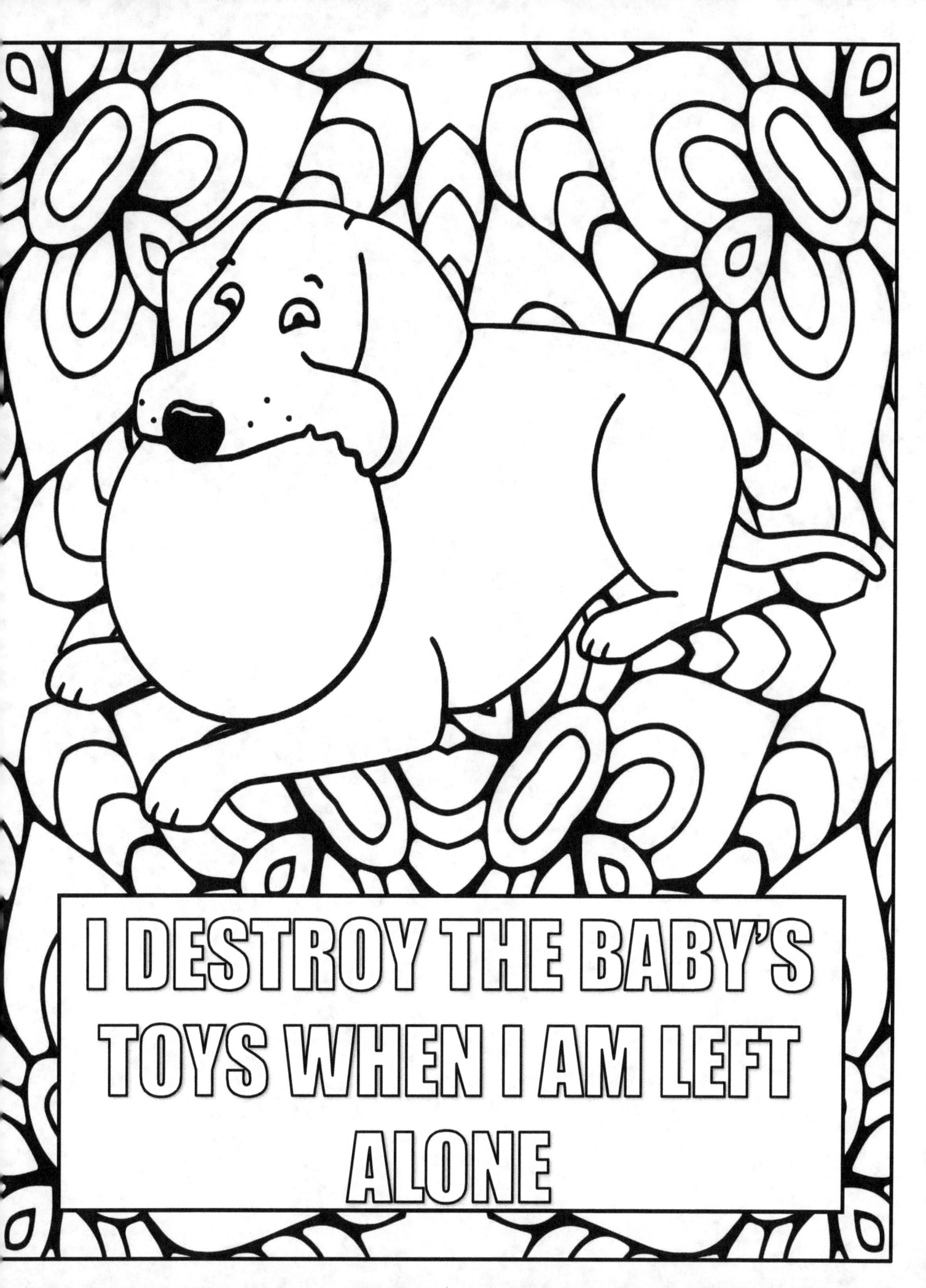

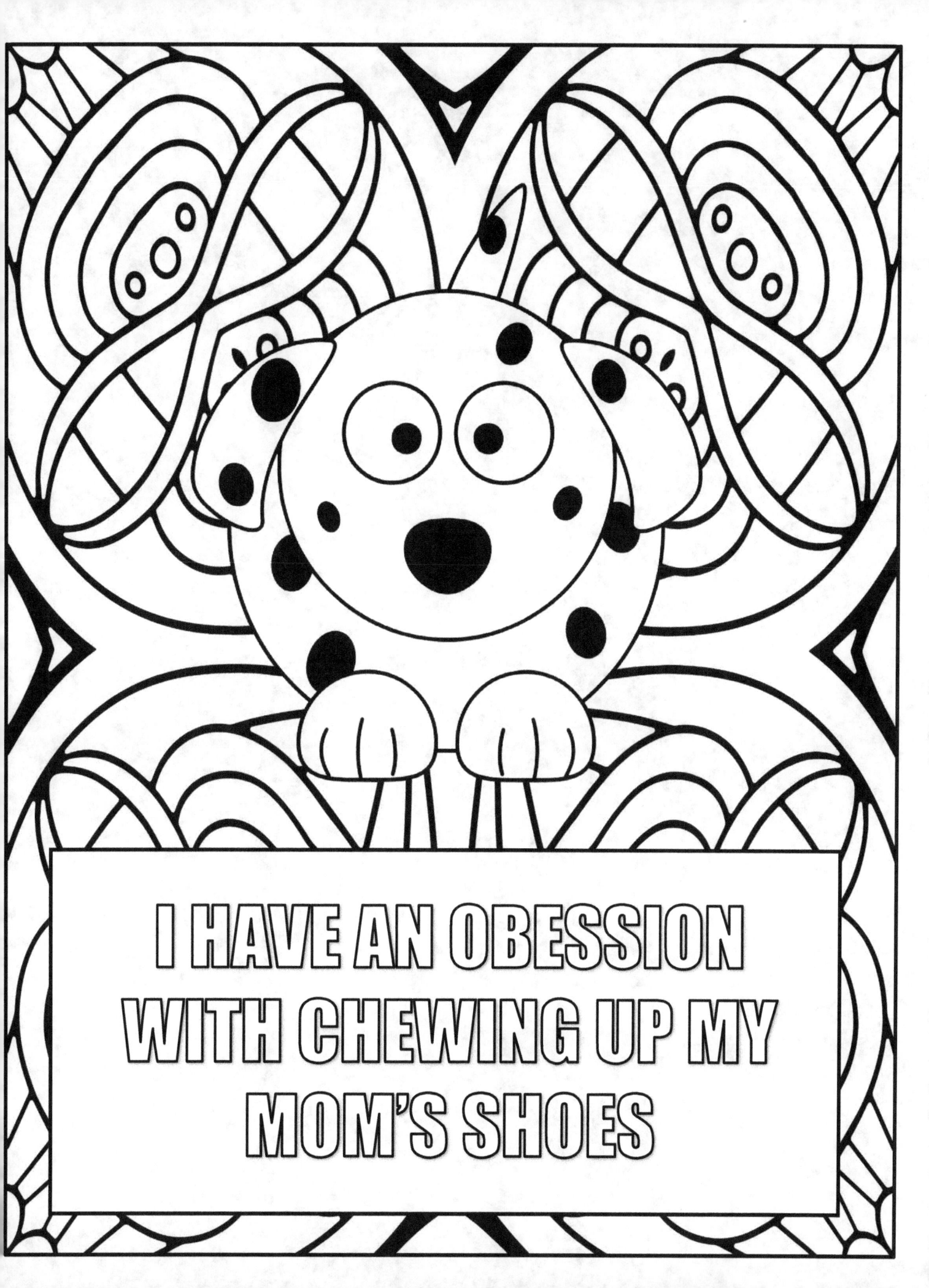

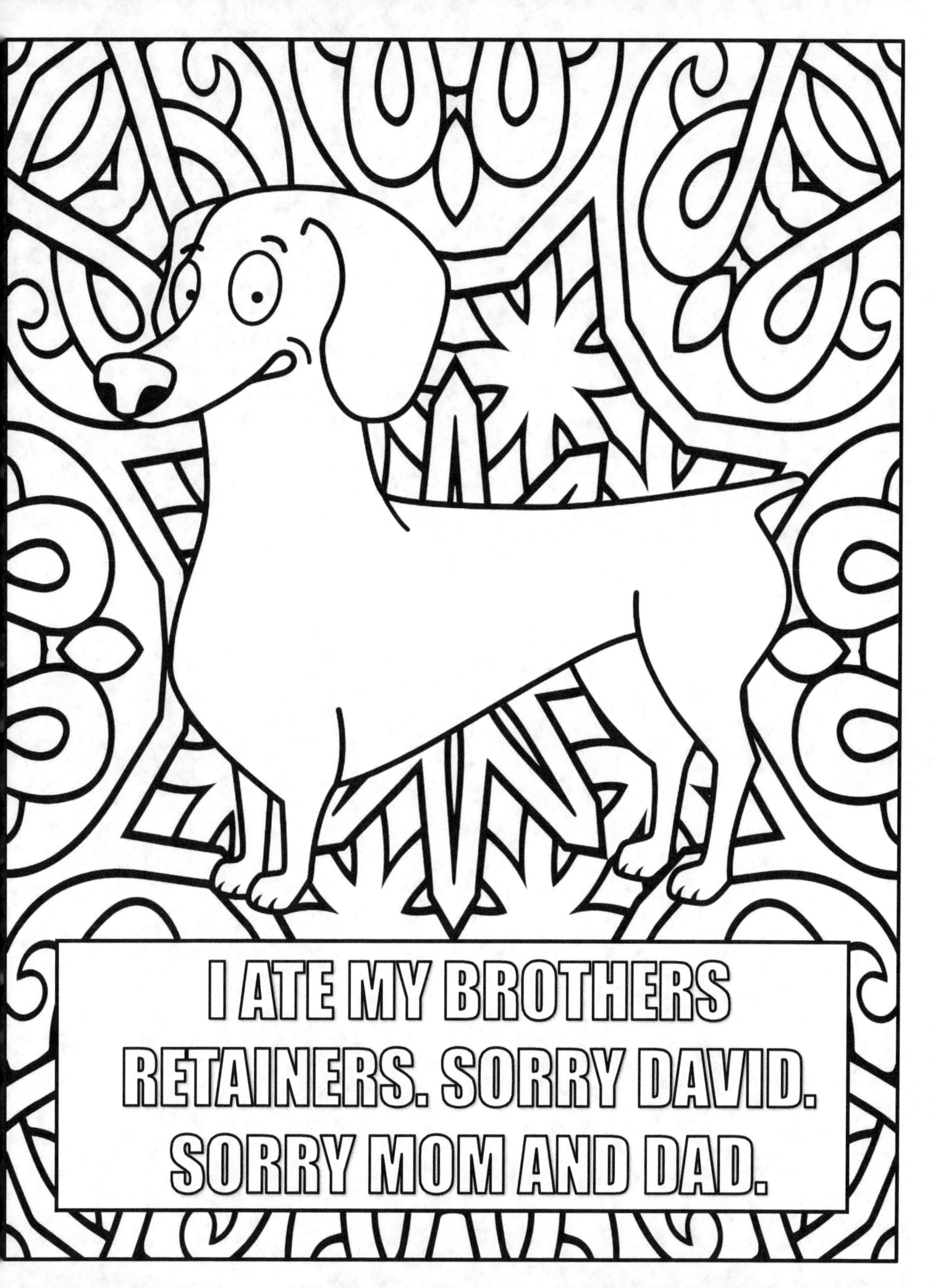

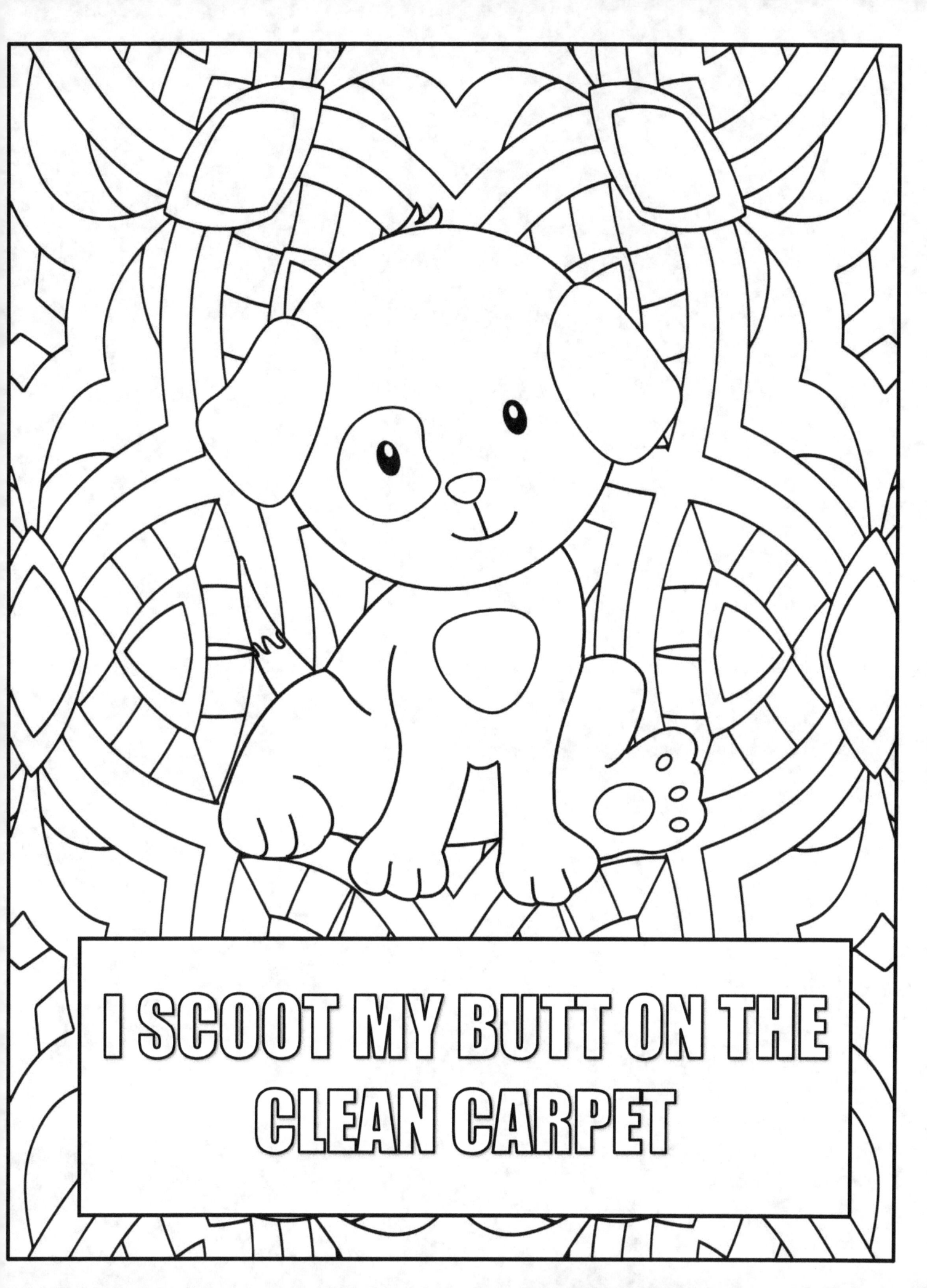

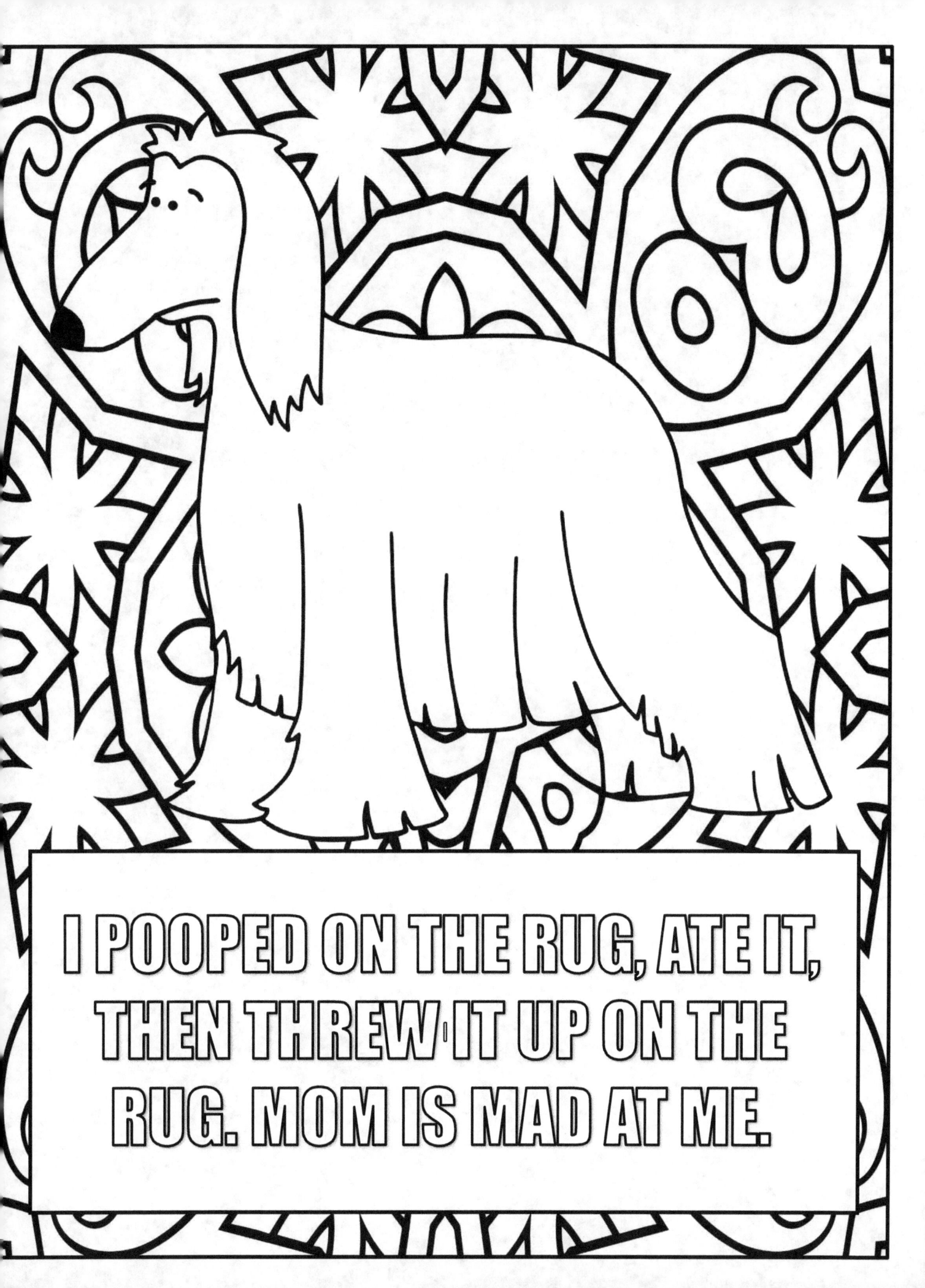

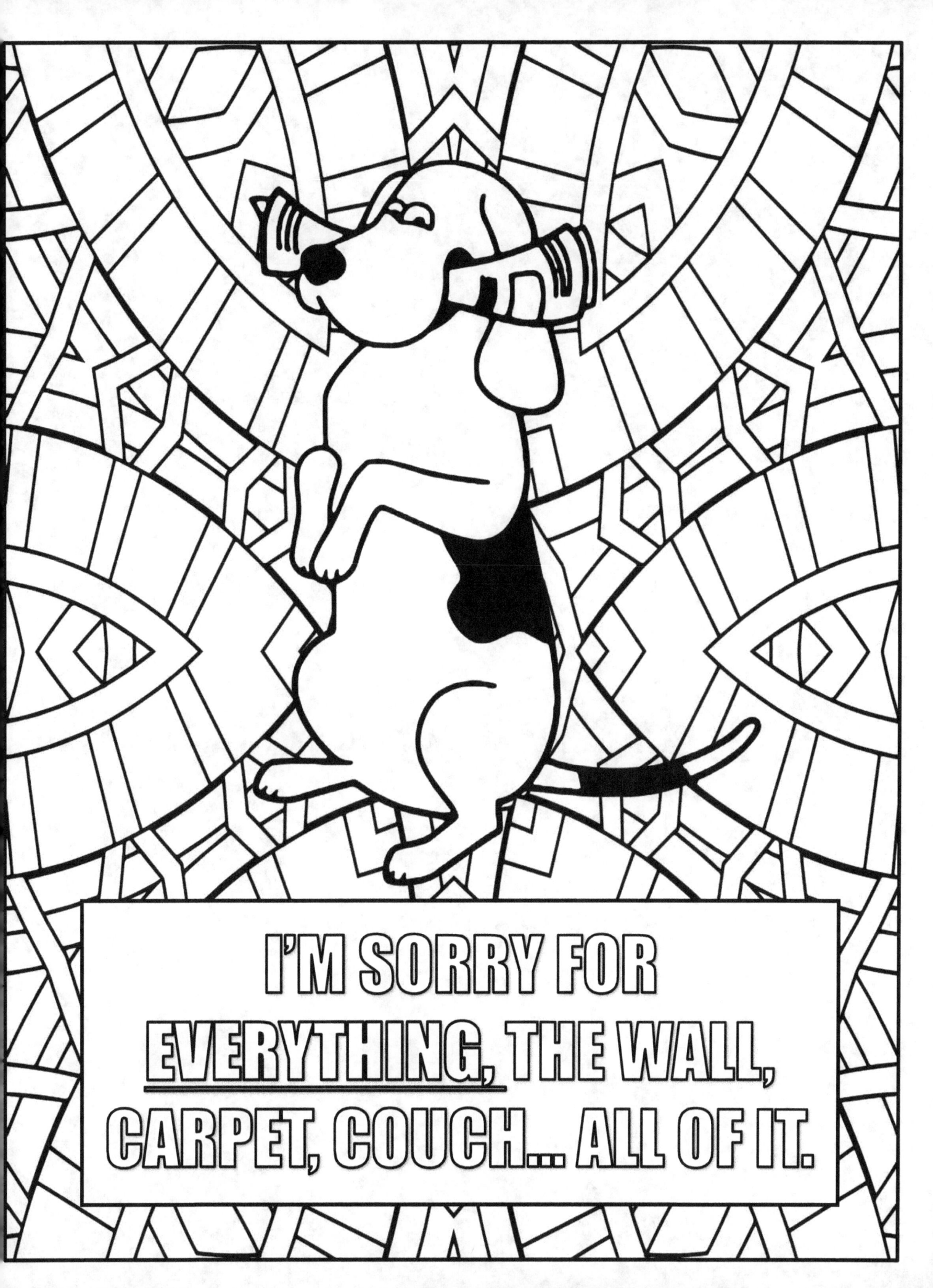

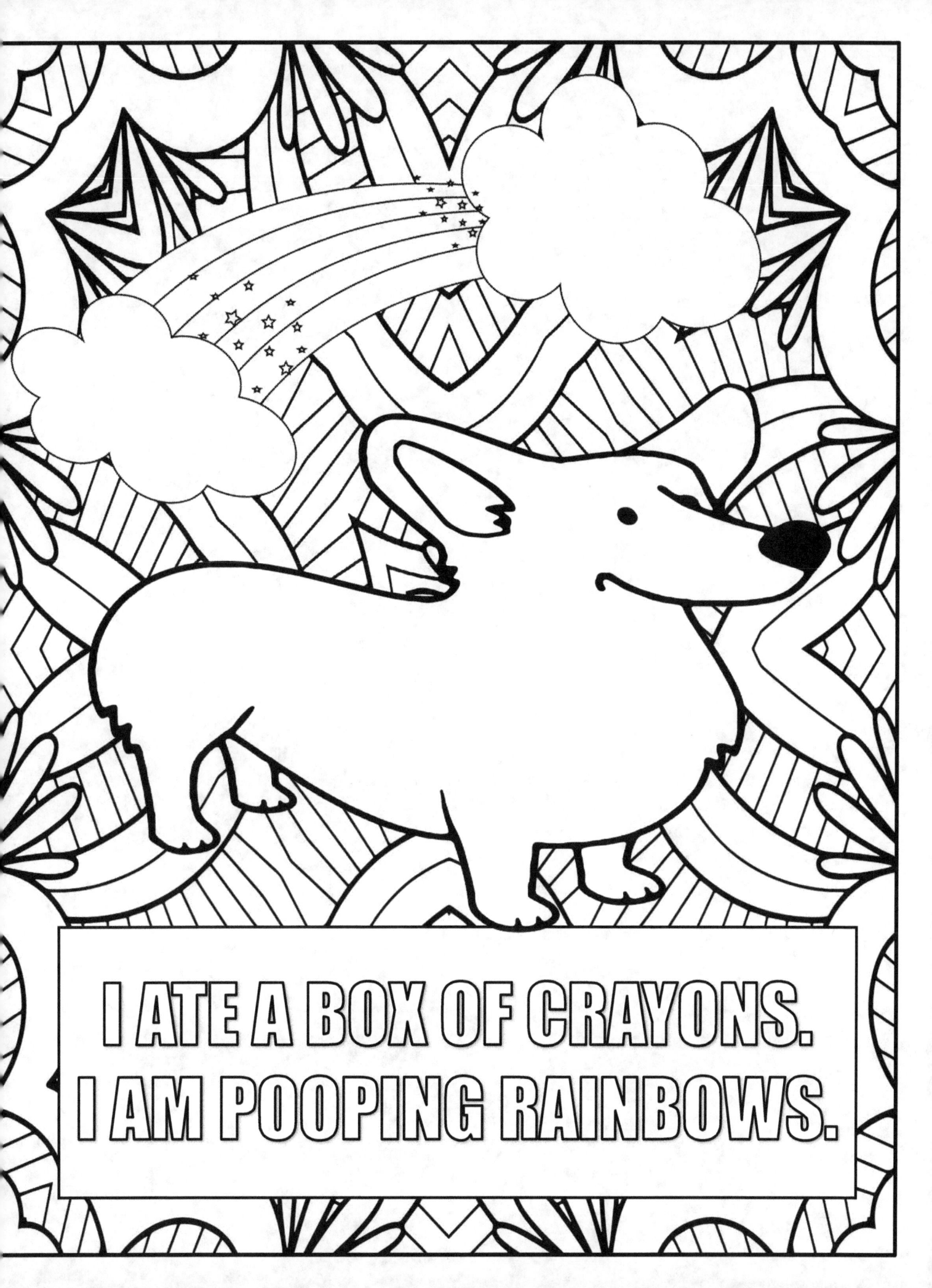

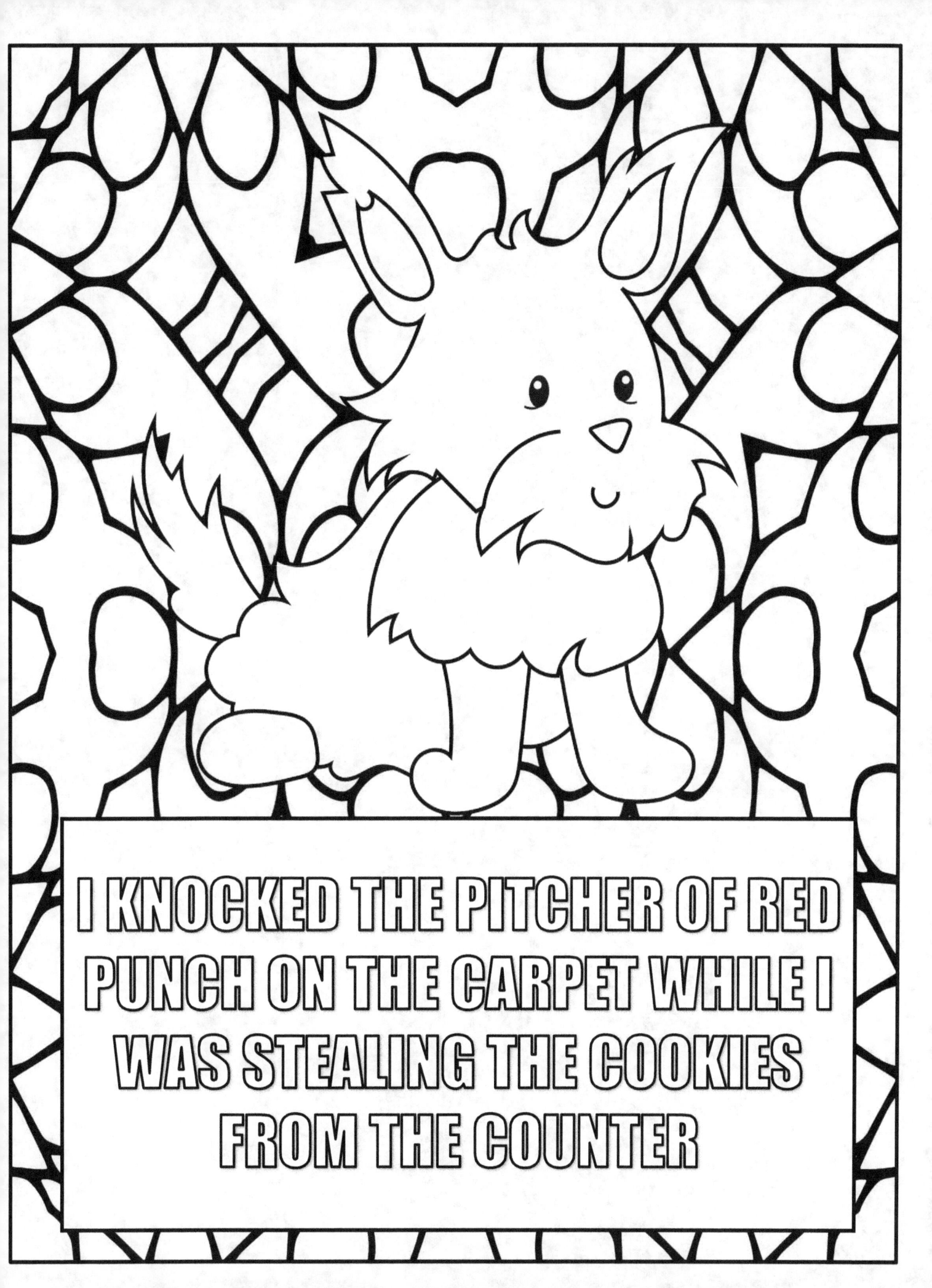

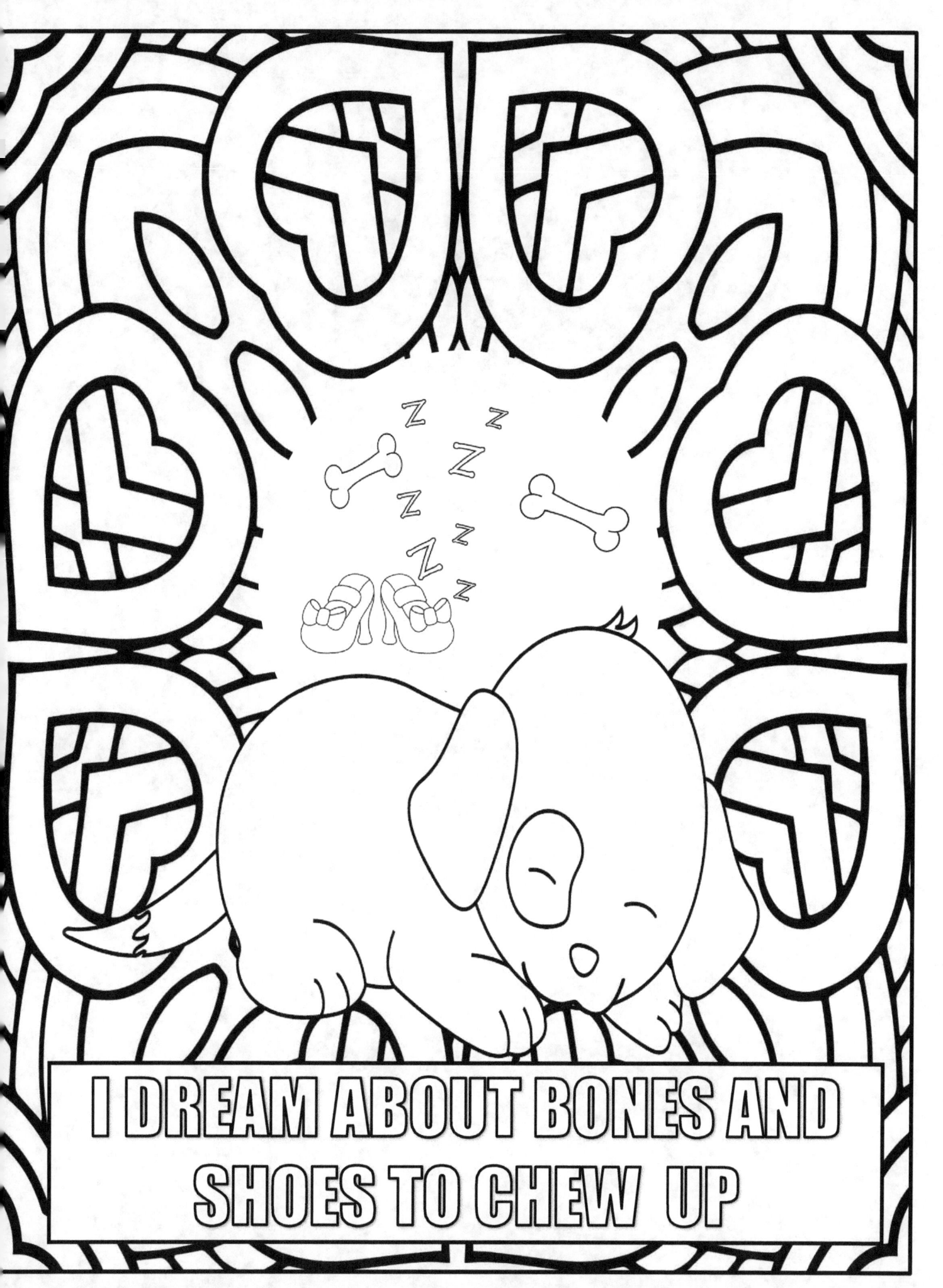

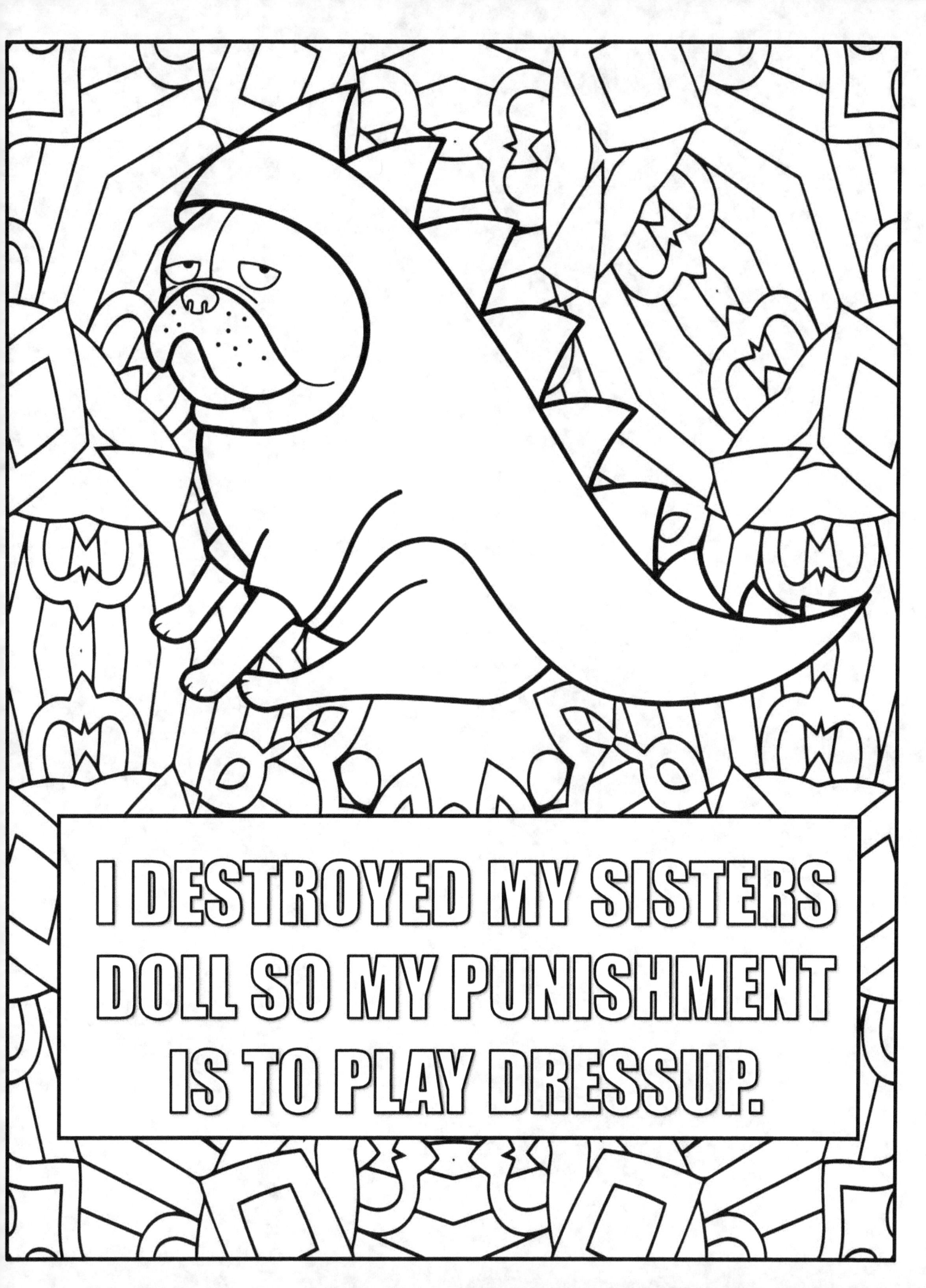

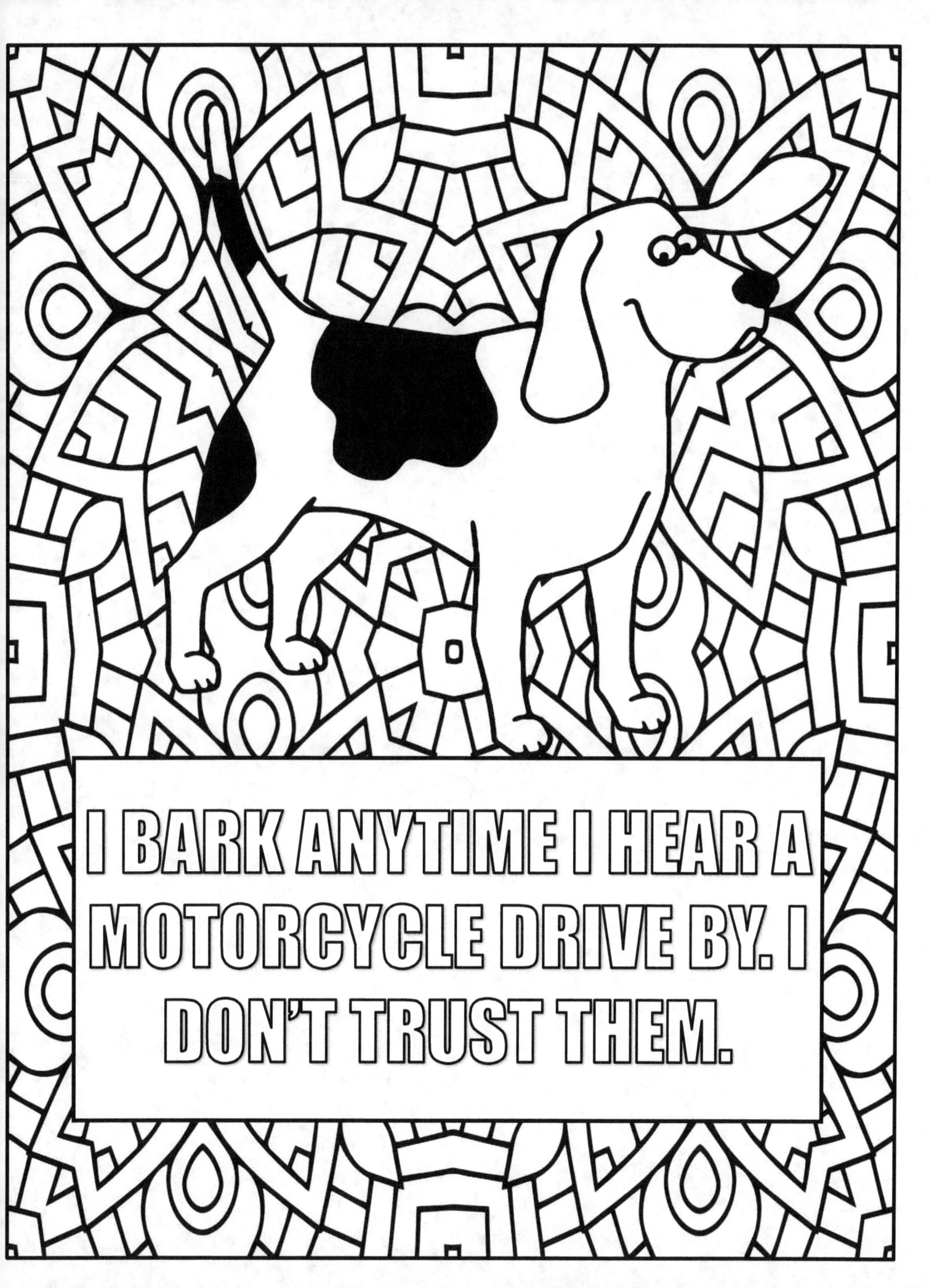

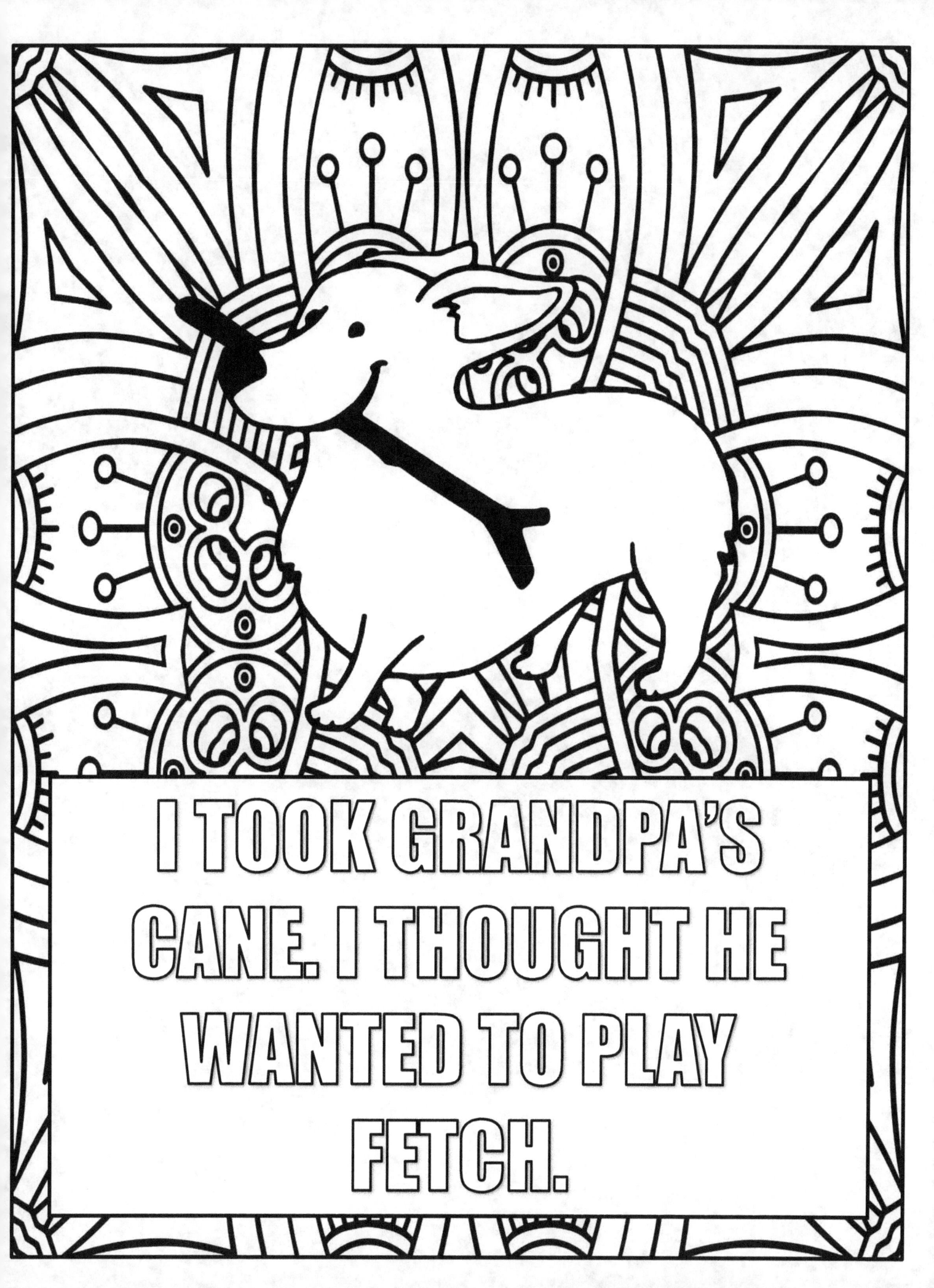

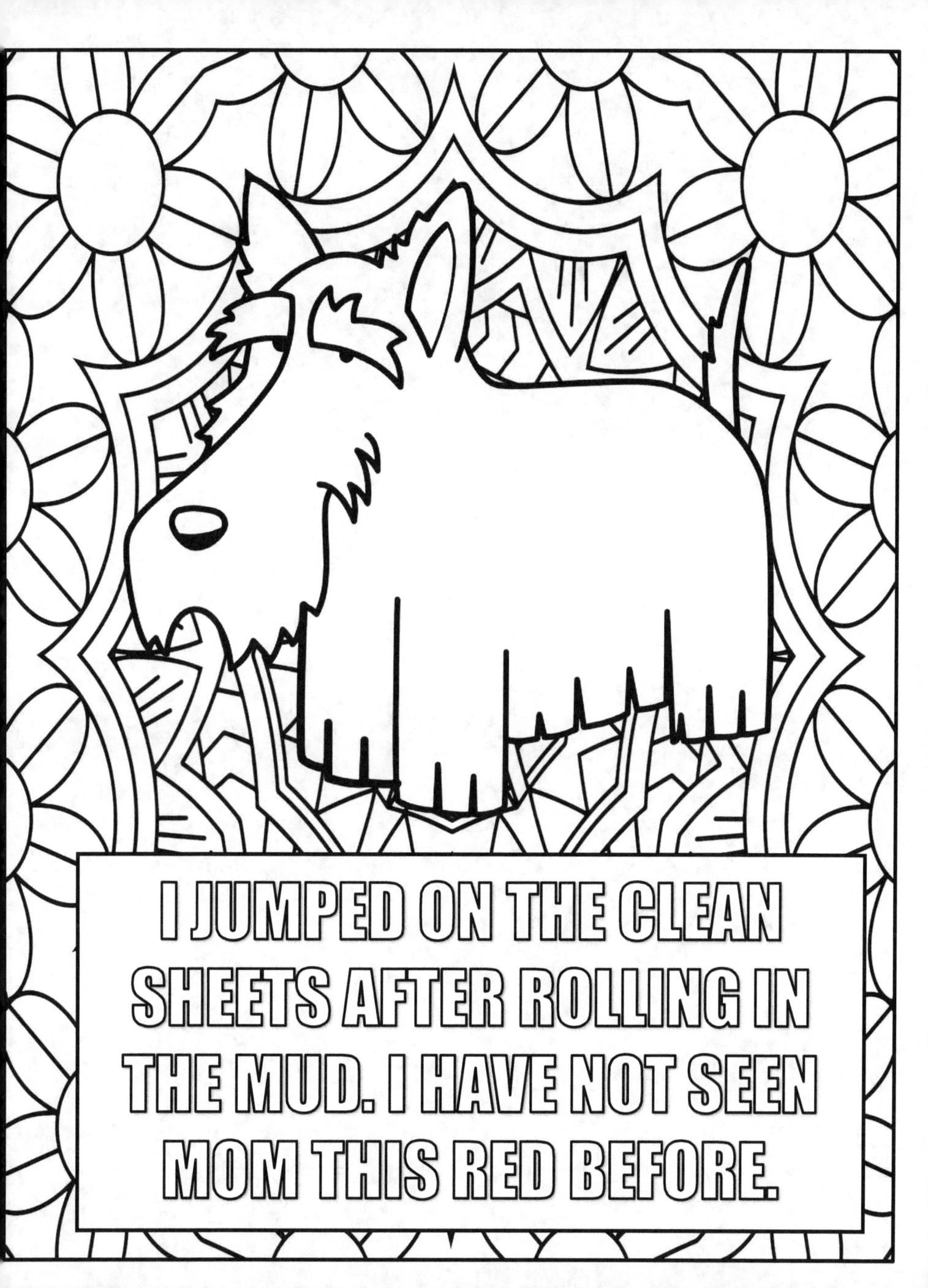

www.ingramcontent.com/pod-product-compliance
Lightning Source LLC
Chambersburg PA
CBHW081658220526
45466CB00009B/2800